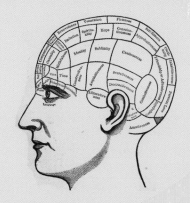

Mind Games

WHAT'S YOUR PERSONALITY?

Facts, Trivia, and Quizzes

calm

thoughtful

Francesca Potts

Lerner Publications ◆ Minneapolis

Lerner Publications Company
A division of Lerner Publishing Group, Inc.
241 First Avenue North
Minneapolis, MN 55401 USA

For reading levels and more information, look up this title at www.lernerbooks.com.

Main body text set in Avenir LT Pro
Typeface provided by Linotype

Library of Congress Cataloging-in-Publication Data

The Cataloging-in-Publication Data for *What's Your Personality?: Facts, Trivia, and Quizzes* is on file at the Library of Congress.
ISBN 978-1-5124-3413-2 (lib. bdg.)
ISBN 978-1-5124-4942-6 (EB pdf)

Manufactured in the United States of America
1-42049-23919-3/8/2017

CONTENTS

Introduction: Explore Your Personality!   4

Chapter 1: That's Ancient History!   6

Chapter 2: Theory Mania   8

Chapter 3: Mega-Famous Myers-Briggs   12

Chapter 4: Four-Letter Learning   18

Chapter 5: Nature or Nurture?   20

Chapter 6: Rainbow Revelations!   24

Chapter 7: Your Unique Personality   26

Draw the Pig!   28

Glossary   30

Further Information   31

Index   32

carefree

Introduction
EXPLORE YOUR PERSONALITY!

Are you adventurous and independent? Are you **creative** and cheerful? Maybe you consider yourself helpful and quiet. All of these words are personality **traits**. Each person has a **unique** personality! Your personality influences how you make decisions, learn, and relate to others.

calm

BEGINNING AT BIRTH

Your personality starts forming from the moment you are born. It continues to develop as you get older. New experiences, relationships, your **environment**, and more all shape your personality. So what does your personality say about you? Keep reading to find out!

It's True!

Humans aren't the only beings with personalities. Animals have them too! Personality traits have been discovered in cats, dogs, birds, and even spiders!

Chapter 1

THAT'S ANCIENT HISTORY!

People have been studying personality since ancient times. Greek physician Hippocrates developed the first known personality theory in 370 CE. It was called the Four Humors theory. It associated personality traits to people's bodily fluids.

thoughtful

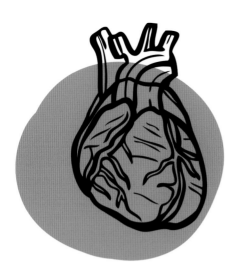

BLOOD, GUTS, AND BILE!

Each of the four humors was associated with a
bodily fluid. Hippocrates believed that the amount
of these fluids a person had in their body
influenced their personality. People with
a lot of blood were **optimistic**. A person
with excess **mucus** was **sluggish**. The
more black **bile** a person had, the
sadder they were. And those with a
lot of yellow bile were angry.

SCIENCE SAYS...

In the 1700s, scientists proved the Four Humors
theory was not true. But many people continued to
use it to study personality in the coming centuries.

Chapter 2

THEORY MANIA

The study of personality exploded in the 1900s. Several **psychologists** formed theories examining different aspects of personality. Many of these theories are still used.

1 2 3

FREUD'S PHILOSOPHIES

Psychologist Sigmund Freud did a great deal of research on the mind in the 1900s. He believed the mind can be broken down into three parts: the ego, the superego, and the id. The id is a person's instincts and wants. The superego is influenced by the rules and morals a person learns. The ego is the **rational** part of a person. It helps balance the id's wants with the superego's rules. Freud believed these three parts work together to create someone's personality.

It's True!

Your personality can help **predict** the types of music you listen to, the types of foods you like, and the types of books you want to read.

BEHAVIORISM

Psychologist John B. Watson developed a theory in 1913 called behaviorism. Watson's theory states that personality does not begin at birth. Instead, he believed personality is a result of a person's environment and experiences. He also believed a person's intelligence is the result of how they were raised and the behaviors they learned.

JUNG: FOUR FUNCTIONS

Psychologist Carl Jung often discussed theories with Freud. In 1923, he developed his own theory on personality. He believed that a person's ego shapes their personality. Jung said the ego has four methods of processing information and making decisions. These are sensing, intuition, thinking, and feeling.

A person displays different traits depending on which functions are most to least dominant.

Chapter 3

MEGA-FAMOUS MYERS-BRIGGS

In the 1940s, Katharine Cook Briggs and her daughter Isabel Briggs Myers expanded Jung's theory to include additional labels. The Myers-Briggs theory is divided into four categories with two parts each.

Energy

Where a person gets energy from plays an important role in how they behave.

EXTRAVERSION
Extraverts get their energy from outside themselves, such as being around people or in an active environment.

INTROVERSION
Introverts get their energy from within, spending time alone or in a quieter environment.

Information

Sensing and intuition refer to the way someone takes in and understands information.

SENSING

Some people prefer to use their physical senses to gather information. This includes seeing, touching, hearing, feeling, tasting, and smelling.

INTUITION

Others prefer to gather information by thinking about patterns and meaning. They trust their instincts to decide what is real.

Decisions

Thinking and feeling are two ways a person makes decisions.

THINKING

People who identify with this category use **logic** to make decisions.

FEELING

People who identify with this category use their values to make decisions.

Structure

These functions describe the way a person approaches life.

JUDGING

People in this category approach life in a structured way. They are often very organized.

PERCEIVING

Some people approach life in an open way. They prefer to be more **flexible**.

POPULAR PERSONALITY TEST

Did you find any similarities between the Myers-Briggs descriptions and yourself? The idea behind this theory is that you are more like one category of each pair than the other. This theory is applied using a test called the Myers-Briggs Type Indicator (MBTI).

thoughtful

Four-Letter Findings

At the end of the MBTI, people learn their four-letter combination. There are sixteen possible combinations. Each one describes traits and behaviors for that type of personality.

Extravert E

Introvert I

Sensing S

Intuition N

Thinking T

Feeling F

Judging J

Perceiving P

ISTP

ENFP

ISFJ

ESTJ

What's Your Myers-Briggs Type?

Have you guessed which Myers-Briggs categories you fit in? Find out if your guesses are correct! Follow the question paths below. On a separate sheet of paper, write down the letters you are led to. What's your four-letter personality type?

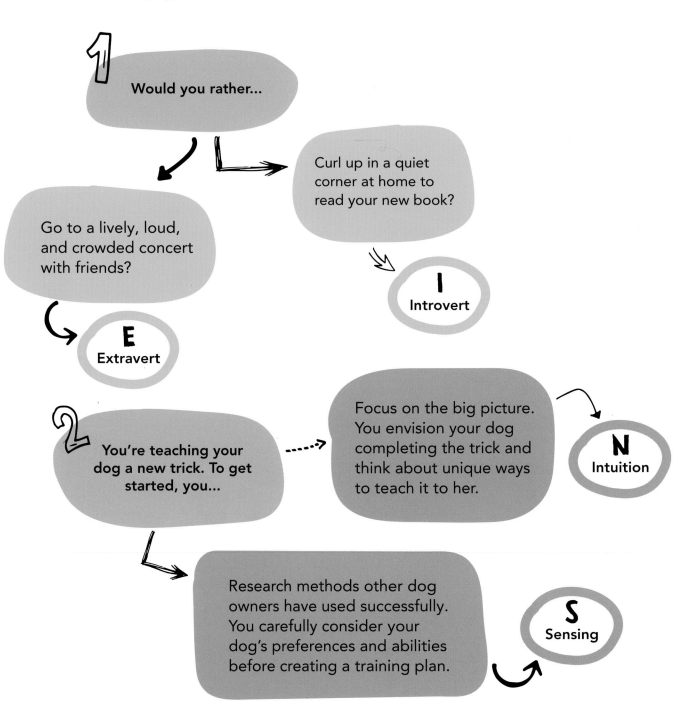

1

Would you rather...

Curl up in a quiet corner at home to read your new book?

I
Introvert

Go to a lively, loud, and crowded concert with friends?

E
Extravert

2

You're teaching your dog a new trick. To get started, you...

Focus on the big picture. You envision your dog completing the trick and think about unique ways to teach it to her.

N
Intuition

Research methods other dog owners have used successfully. You carefully consider your dog's preferences and abilities before creating a training plan.

S
Sensing

3 Your family is driving to the store, and your siblings are arguing over whose turn it is to ride in the middle seat. You...

 Discuss who last rode in the middle to determine correctly whose turn it is now. You helped your siblings set rules about this long ago for this reason!

T
Thinking

Try to create peace and harmony. You consider your siblings' feelings as you help resolve the problem.

F
Feeling

4 Your teacher assigns a book report that is due next month. You...

Imagine ways to make the assignment fun. You think about creating a colorful poster instead of a paper report, or putting on a play about the book's plot.

P
Perceiving

Choose a book and begin making to-do lists and researching right after school. You'd rather get the report done early than worry about it for weeks!

J
Judging

YOUR TYPE:

? ? ? ?
___ ___ ___ ___

IS IT SCIENCE?

Research has found that the Myers-Briggs test is not reliable. But it is still used by millions of people each year. The test can be a fun way to discover more about what makes you *you*!

Chapter 4
FOUR-LETTER LEARNING

Did you figure out your Myers-Briggs type from the quiz on pages 16 and 17? On the following page, find the four letters you identified with from the quiz. Do they match up with how you like to learn new skills and information?

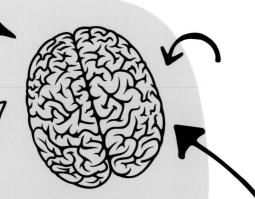

Setting

E (Extravert): You learn best with others, such as group discussion or studying with friends.

I (Introvert): You learn best independently. This includes reading, quietly studying, and writing.

Receiving Information

S (Sensing): You prefer to receive information in an organized manner. You like step-by-step instructions.

N (Intuition): You prefer to receive information about the big picture first and then facts. You like to learn using problem-solving activities.

Interpreting Information

T (Thinking): You prefer to use logic and research when learning.

F (Feeling): You learn best when you can relate something to a personal experience or emotion.

Completing Projects

J (Judging): You learn best with clear instructions and deadlines.

P (Perceiving): You like work that can be completed in many ways and has many possible outcomes.

Chapter 5
NATURE OR NURTURE?

Where does personality come from? Were you born with it? Or does your personality develop as you experience things? This is the debate of nature versus nurture.

IT'S NATURE!

Many scientists believe nature forms your personality. They say the genes you were born with determine your physical characteristics, like the color of your eyes or your height. Some scientists believe genes also determine your behavior, choices, and preferences.

NOPE, IT'S NURTURE!

Other scientists believe in the nurture theory. They say your personality is influenced by your experiences, education, and upbringing. They argue that behaviors and preferences change over time depending on what a person has learned and experienced.

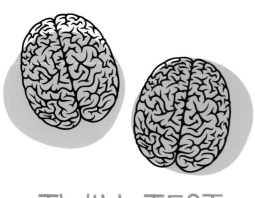

TWIN TEST

One argument for the nurture theory involves identical twins. Identical twins share the same **genetics**. This means that if personality were based on genes alone, identical twins should have similar personalities. Research has shown that identical twins sometimes have similar preferences or behavior. But they do not have the same personalities! They may act, learn, and make choices differently.

YOU DECIDE!

So, which theory is correct, nature or nurture? Most researchers say personality is a result of both genes and experiences. You can decide which you think makes you *you*!

Does Birth Order Affect Personality?

Do you have brothers and sisters? Are you the youngest, oldest, or in the middle? Maybe you are an only child. Some researchers believe your birth order affects your personality. Take this quiz to find out!

Look at the words below. On a separate sheet of paper, copy the four words that sound the most like you.

peacemaker	successful	carefree	mature
responsible	confident	leader	outgoing
risk-taker	social	ambitious	perfectionist
independent	rebellious	charming	thoughtful

Check the lists below for the words you chose. Do they fall under your correct birth order?

Oldest:
responsible
leader
ambitious
successful

Middle:
peacemaker
social
rebellious
thoughtful

Youngest:
outgoing
carefree
risk-taker
charming

Only Child:
mature
perfectionist
confident
independent

Chapter 6

RAINBOW REVELATIONS!

Some researchers think colors can determine your personality!
The Color Code Personality test involves choosing which colors
draw you in. Each color relates to different personality traits
and behaviors. It is a simple test. But the answers can reveal a
lot about your personality!

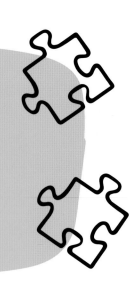

What's Your Personality Color?

The Color Code Personality test describes personality in relation to a person's color preferences. Do you think it would work on you?

Choose a color below. Find out what your choice says about your personality. Then quiz your friends to see if their color choices match their personalities!

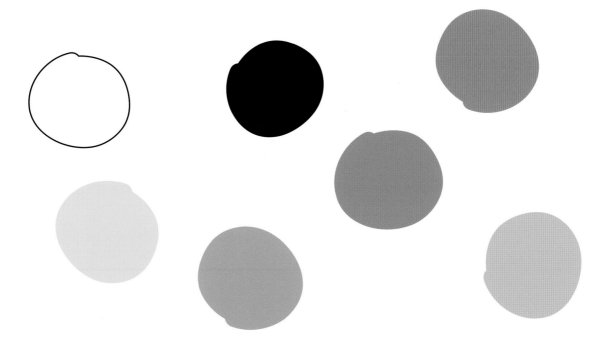

IF YOU CHOSE:

White or Black:
You are very organized and neat. You are great at memorizing things! You are a rule follower.

Orange:
You are cheerful and happy! You like to be around people and may be a class clown.

Red or Pink:
You are brave! You are also emotional and a great listener.

Yellow:
You are hardworking and smart. You respect others' opinions. You can have a hard time making decisions.

Green:
You are a natural leader. You are focused and make decisions easily.

Chapter 7

YOUR UNIQUE PERSONALITY

Studying personality is a complicated task. Many scientists disagree about which personality theory is correct. One thing everyone agrees on is that no one has the same exact personality as someone else!

KEEP EXPLORING!

Taking personality quizzes and learning about theories can be a fun way to learn about yourself. There are other ways to discover what makes you an individual. Self-discovery can also include studying dreams, astrological signs, and more. Have fun learning more about what makes you unique!

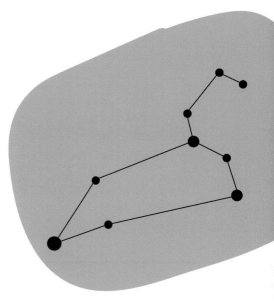

Draw the Pig!

The Pig Drawing Analysis is a fun, and sometimes silly, personality test. Try this test alone. Then test it out on family and friends!

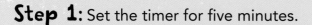

Materials:
- timer or stopwatch
- sheet of paper
- pencil

Step 1: Set the timer for five minutes.

Step 2: Draw a pig on the sheet of paper. It can have as many or few details as you want to add.

Step 3: When the time is up, review the lists below. What does your pig say about your personality?

Pig Orientation

Facing left:
You like tradition and have a good memory. You are also friendly and outgoing!

Facing right:
You are creative and active. But you do not have the best memory!

Facing forward:
You tell it like it is. You can often understand both sides of an argument.

Pig Location

Near the top of the page:
You are a positive thinker.

Near the bottom of the page:
You can be a **negative** thinker.

In the center of the page:
You are a **realistic** thinker.

Pig Legs

Four legs:
You are confident in your opinions. But you can be stubborn!

Fewer than four legs:
You are sometimes uncertain. This may also mean you are going through a period of major change.

Number of Details

Great detail (includes eyelashes, teeth, skin patterns, etc.):
You analyze things carefully. But some people may see you as distrustful.

Few details (basic outline of the pig with little else):
You are a risk-taker. You care more about the big picture than little details.

Pig Ears and Tail

Ears
The larger the ears, the better listener you are.

Tail
The longer the pig's tail, the happier you are with your personal relationships.

GLOSSARY

bile: a greenish-yellow fluid made by the liver and stored in the gallbladder that helps you digest your food

confident: having a strong belief in your own abilities

creative: skillful at using your imagination and making new things

environment: all the things that are part of your life and have an effect on it, such as events, your family, and where you live

flexible: easily able to change

genetics: the makeup of genes in a living being

logic: good or valid thinking or reasoning

mucus: a thick, slimy liquid coating the inside of the nose and throat

negative: focusing on only the bad side of something or someone

optimistic: believing things will always turn out well or for the best

predict: to say what will happen in the future

psychologists: people who study human emotions, behaviors, and minds

rational: logical and sensible, not emotional

realistic: seeing things as they really are

rebellious: defying or resisting management

sluggish: moving slowly and without energy

traits: qualities or characteristics

unique: unlike anyone or anything else

FURTHER INFORMATION

It's My Life

http://pbskids.org/itsmylife/family/birthorder/index.html

Learn about how being the youngest, oldest, middle, or only child in your family can affect your personality.

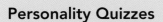

Oglethorpe, Alice. *Personality Patterns Quiz Book*. Middleton, WI: American Girl Publishing, 2013.

This book is full of cool and surprising quizzes that can help you learn all about you!

Personality Quizzes

http://kids.nationalgeographic.com/explore/adventure_pass/personality-quizzes

Discover which baby animal, explorer, and musical instrument you are and much more by taking the fun quizzes on this website.

Quiz: What's Your Job Personality?

http://www.kidzworld.com/quiz/2815-quiz-whats-your-job-personality

Find out what career best matches your personality!

Zuchora-Walske, Christine. *Your Head Shape Reveals Your Personality! Science's Biggest Mistakes about the Human Body*. Minneapolis, MN: Lerner Publications Company, 2015.

Read all about the odd ideas scientists once had about the human body, and how their thoughts have changed.

INDEX

animal personalities, 5

behaviorism theory, 10
birth order, 23
Briggs, Katharine
    Cook, 12

Color Code
    Personality test,
    24–25

Four Humors theory,
    6–7
Freud, Sigmund, 9, 11

Hippocrates, 6–7

history, 6–11

introduction, 4–5

Jung, Carl, 11–12

learning, 18–19

Myers, Isabel Briggs,
    12
Myers-Briggs theory,
    12–19

nature, 20–22
nurture, 20–22

Pig Drawing Analysis,
    28–29
predictive personality,
    9
psychologists, 8–11

quizzes, 16–17, 23, 25

self-understanding, 27

twins, 22

Watson, John B., 10

Photo Acknowledgments

The images in this book are used with the permission of: Design elements and doodles © Fears/Shutterstock.com, kostolom3000/Shutterstock.com, Macrovector/Shutterstock.com, mhatzapa/Shutterstock.com, nellysembiring/Shutterstock.com, Nikolaeva/Shutterstock.com, Photoraidz/Shutterstock.com, Sashatigar/Shutterstock.com, Tond Van Graphcraft/Shutterstock.com, Vector Tradition/Shutterstock.com, and whitemomo/Shutterstock.com; © cjp/iStockphoto.com, pp. 1 (left), 4 (middle); © PeopleImages/iStockphoto.com, p. 1 (right); © Africa Studio/Shutterstock.com, p. 3; © UMB-O/Shutterstock.com, p. 4 (top); © Wavebreakmedia/iStockphoto.com, p. 4 (bottom); © Maya Kruchankova/Shutterstock.com, p. 5 (top); © Syda Productions/Shutterstock.com, p. 5 (bottom); © ZU_09/iStockphoto.com, p. 6; © altanaka/Shutterstock.com, p. 7 (top); © CHALITSA HONGTONG/Shutterstock.com, p. 7 (bottom); © monkeybusinessimages/iStockphoto.com, pp. 8, 10 (bottom); © Max Halberstadt/Wikimedia Commons, p. 9 (top); © stacey_newman/iStockphoto.com, p. 9 (bottom); © The Johns Hopkins Gazette/Wikimedia Commons, p. 10 (top); © Ortsmuseum Zollikon/Wikimedia Commons, p. 11 (top); © ArtMarie/iStockphoto.com, p. 11 (bottom); © kali9/iStockphoto.com, p. 14 (top); © Photographee.eu/Shutterstock.com, p. 14 (bottom); © THEGIFT777/iStockphoto.com, p. 18; © upslim/Shutterstock.com, p. 20; © Piti Tan/Shutterstock.com, p. 21 (top); © omgimages/iStockphoto.com, p. 21 (bottom); © Syda Productions/Shutterstock.com, p. 22 (top); © Andy Dean Photography/Shutterstock.com, p. 22 (bottom); © holbox/Shutterstock.com, p. 24; © XiXinXing/iStockphoto.com, p. 26; © Lapina/Shutterstock.com, p. 27 (top); © omgimages/iStockphoto.com, p. 27 (bottom); © Maica/iStockphoto.com, p. 29.

Front cover: © Stone36/Shutterstock.com (top, left); © gradyreese/iStockphoto.com (middle, left); © Mari/iStockphoto.com (middle, right); © PeopleImages/iStockphoto.com (bottom, left).

Back cover: © Maica/iStockphoto.com (top); © Wavebreakmedia/iStockphoto.com (middle); © ArtMarie/iStockphoto.com (bottom).